CROSS STITCH
PATTERNS

A Journey Through 30 Natural Wonders

Lily Ann

Contents

INTRODUCTION   4

PATTERN 1
Thundering Waterfall of the Border   8

PATTERN 2
Geysers and Wilderness of Wyoming   11

PATTERN 3
Slot Canyons of Arizona   14

PATTERN 4
Ancient Pyramids of the Maya   17

PATTERN 5
Lungs of the Earth in Brazil   20

PATTERN 6
Archipelago of Evolution   23

PATTERN 7
Rapa Nui's Ancient Guardians   26

PATTERN 8
Circle of Ancient Stones   29

PATTERN 9
Alpine Majesty of Switzerland   32

PATTERN 10
Thundering Curtain of Water   35

PATTERN 11
Endless Plains of the Tanzanian Wild   38

PATTERN 12
Golden Crescent Shore of Sydney   41

PATTERN 13
Scenic Coastal Journey of Victoria   44

PATTERN 14
Limestone Spires of Nambung   47

PATTERN 15
Jagged Peaks of Queenstown   50

PATTERN 16
Mystic Spheres of Moeraki   53

PATTERN 17
Emerald Isle of the Pacific   56

PATTERN 18
Volcanic Isle of Antarctica   59

PATTERN 19
Sacred Summit of Japan   62

PATTERN 20
Limestone Jewels of Vietnam   65

PATTERN 21
Island of Gods in Indonesia   68

PATTERN 22
Buddhist Majesty in Java   71

PATTERN 23
Land of Dragons in Indonesia   74

PATTERN 24
Lion Rock Fortress of Lanka   77

PATTERN 25
Volcanic Beauty of Jeju   80

PATTERN 26
Dragon's Backbone of China   83

PATTERN 27
Gateway to the Earth's Crown   86

PATTERN 28
Fairy Chimneys and Hidden Valleys   89

PATTERN 29
Salt Lake of Tranquility   92

PATTERN 30
Colorful Underwater Paradise   95

THREAD CONVERSION   98

Introduction

Welcome to the world of cross stitch! If you're just starting out, you might be wondering about all the tools and materials you'll need. Don't worry; I've got you covered. Let's walk through the essentials to get you stitching in no time.

Materials and Tools

Fabric

Cross stitch is typically done on a type of fabric called 'Aida', which is ideal for beginners. Aida comes in various sizes, referred to by 'count' (ct). The count number tells you how many squares there are per inch. For starters, I recommend using 14-count Aida. For those looking to explore beyond Aida, Evenweave and Linen are excellent alternatives. These fabrics typically come in higher counts, such as 28 or 32, and are often stitched over two threads.

Embroidery Floss

This is usually made of cotton and comes in skeins. Each skein is made up of six strands, but for most patterns on 14-count Aida, you'll use only two or three strands at a time.

Needle

You'll need a tapestry needle. For 14-count Aida, a size 24 needle works best.

Hoop or Frame

A hoop or frame isn't essential, but it can help you by keeping the fabric tight and easy to work with. They come in different sizes: small hoops (4-6 inches) are great for little projects, while larger ones suit bigger pieces.

Additional Tools

Use sharp scissors for cutting embroidery floss, a needle minder to secure your needle, and a thread organizer for managing multiple colors.

Getting Started

Preparing the Fabric

Before you begin stitching, you should cut your fabric to the desired size, allowing a few inches on each side beyond the actual design area. This extra fabric makes it easier to handle or frame your finished work.

Once cut, consider edging your fabric to prevent fraying. You can do this by sewing a simple zigzag stitch along the edges, or even applying a bit of fray-check solution. After your edges are secure, fold your fabric into quarters to find the center. This central point is a great place to start stitching, ensuring your design is perfectly centered.

Threading the Needle

Cut a length of embroidery floss about 18 inches long—this length prevents tangling and is manageable to work with. Most designs call for using two strands of floss, so separate out the required strands and thread them through the needle's eye. Leave a small tail and you're ready to start stitching.

Starting Your First Stitch

To begin, you have a few options for securing your thread. One method is to start with a knot, or you can leave a short tail of thread on the backside of your fabric, securing it beneath your initial stitches to keep the reverse side neat and flat.

Alternatively, for a cleaner start, use the **loop method**: fold one strand of thread in half, thread the folded end through your needle to create a loop on the opposite end, and start your stitch. As you pull the needle back to the front, catch the loop to secure the thread without knots, keeping the back tidy.

Loop Method

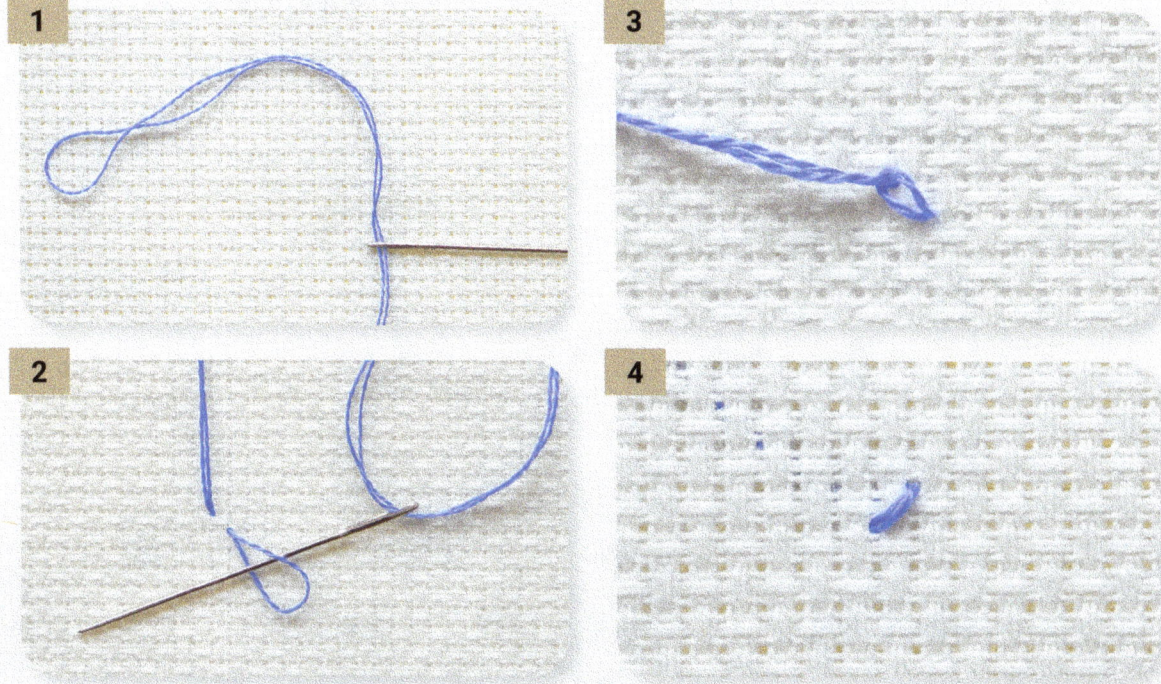

Basic Techniques

The Cross Stitch (X)

The basic unit of cross stitch is the 'X'. Begin by bringing the needle up from the back at either the bottom left or bottom right of a square. If starting from the bottom left, go down at the top right to form the first slash; then insert the needle at the bottom right and exit at the top left to complete the 'X'. Alternatively, start from the bottom right, go down at the top left for the first slash, and then from the bottom left to the top right. Whichever starting point you choose, ensure all your top stitches slant in the same direction for a uniform appearance.

You can use the English or Danish method of stitching. The English method completes each 'X' one at a time, preventing thread stretch on the visible back of the fabric. The Danish method stitches all the first slashes in a row (/ / / /) and then completes each 'X' (X X X X), which is quicker and conserves thread.

Finishing Threads

To finish a thread, weave the end under existing stitches on the back of the fabric without piercing the front. Secure it by pulling through several times before trimming the excess. This keeps the back of your work tidy.

Stitching Over Two Threads

Evenweave and Linen fabrics have a more open and uniform weave than Aida. They are made up of evenly spaced threads running vertically and horizontally. When you "stitch over two threads," you are passing the needle over two fabric threads each time you make a stitch. This means that instead of going into every single hole between the threads (as you would with Aida), you skip one thread each time. This creates a larger stitch.

English Method (Top), Danish Method (Bottom)

1

2

Finishing Threads

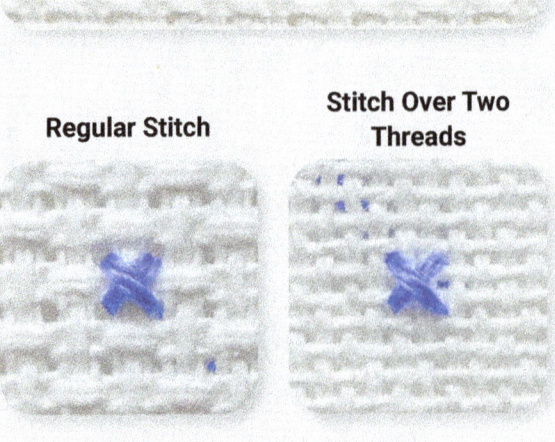

Regular Stitch　　**Stitch Over Two Threads**

Reading Patterns

Grids and Counts

The pattern is typically divided into grids, often 10x10 blocks of squares, making it easier to count and follow. Each square on the grid represents a single cross stitch on the fabric. For clarity and ease, tackle the pattern one block at a time, ensuring accuracy in stitch counts and color placements.

Identifying the Center

Most patterns will have marks indicating the center of the design, usually noted with arrows or lines along the pattern grid. Starting at the center ensures your design is evenly placed and has adequate fabric on all sides for framing.

Symbols and Key (Legend)

Each symbol on a stitch chart corresponds to a specific color of thread. Before starting, familiarize yourself with the key, which lists symbols alongside their respective thread colors and numbers. This is your roadmap, guiding you through each color change and stitch placement.

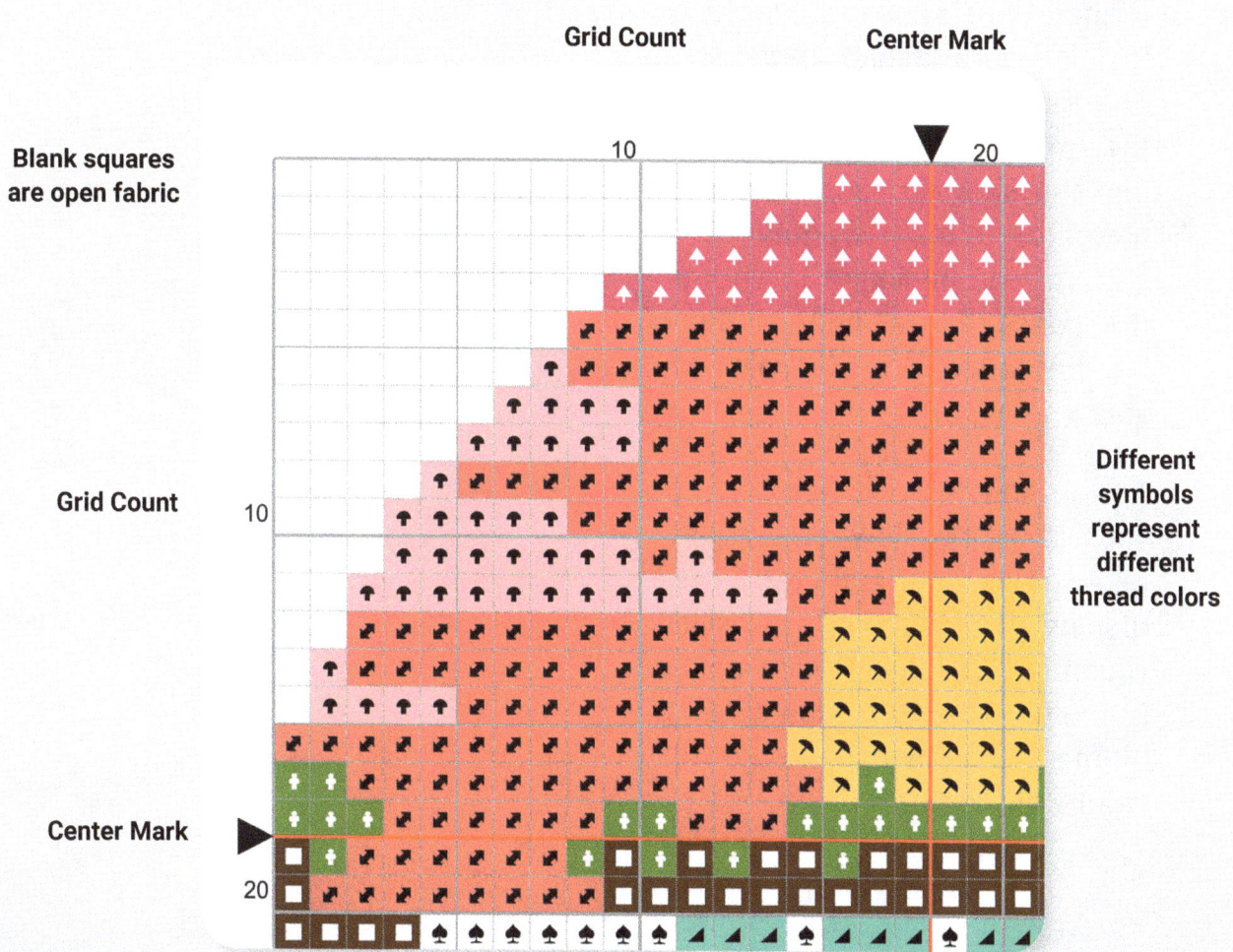

> **PATTERN 1**

Thundering Waterfall of the Border

Niagara Falls

Niagara Falls is one of those places that leaves a lasting impression. The roar of the cascading water, the mist that dances in the air, and the sheer scale of it all—it's nature at its most dramatic. This pattern was designed to capture that sense of awe and movement, bringing a touch of the falls into your stitching.

As you work through each section, you'll see the flow and energy take shape, echoing the rhythm of rushing water. Whether it reminds you of a past adventure or inspires future travels, this design offers a moment of connection to the wild beauty of the world

Quick Facts

» Straddling the border of New York, USA, and Ontario, Canada.

» This majestic waterfall has the highest flow rate of any in North America.

» It's been a filming location for many movies and even a backdrop for daring tightrope walks.

Design Size
» 76x76 stitches

Finished Size
» On 14 ct fabric: 5.4 x 5.4 inches (13.8 x 13.8 cm)

Hoop
» Use a 6-inch (15.2 cm) hoop for stitching and display. A 5.5-inch (13.9 cm) hoop is an option for a snug display fit.

Fabric
» Aida: 14 ct
» Evenweave or Linen: 28 ct (stitched over 2 threads)
» Color: White or Ivory

Thread
» Type: DMC Six-strand embroidery floss
» Usage: Stitch with 2 strands
» Length: See Symbol Key

PATTERN 2

Geysers and Wilderness of Wyoming

Yellowstone

Welcome to the wilds of Wyoming! The landscape is a mix of green meadows, bubbling mud pots, and peaceful lakes. You might even spot an American bison grazing in the distance, a true symbol of this wild land.

As you work on your cross-stitch pattern, let the simple charm of this wild place inspire you. Each stitch brings you closer to capturing the essence of this special area, where the power of nature and peaceful moments come together beautifully.

Quick Facts

» Located in the northwest corner of Wyoming, with parts extending into Montana and Idaho.

» Hosts a diverse range of wildlife, including American bison, elk, and grizzly bears.

Design Size
» 76x76 stitches

Finished Size
» On 14 ct fabric: 5.4 x 5.4 inches (13.8 x 13.8 cm)

Hoop
» Use a 6-inch (15.2 cm) hoop for stitching and display. A 5.5-inch (13.9 cm) hoop is an option for a snug display fit.

Fabric
» Aida: 14 ct
» Evenweave or Linen: 28 ct (stitched over 2 threads)
» Color: White or Ivory

Thread
» Type: DMC Six-strand embroidery floss
» Usage: Stitch with 2 strands
» Length: See Symbol Key

	DMC 310	DMC 958	DMC 905	DMC 801	DMC 954	DMC 434	DMC Ecru
Yards	11.8	2.9	10.3	20.5	23.8	3.9	18.5
Meters	10.8	2.7	9.4	18.7	21.8	3.6	16.9

PATTERN 3

Slot Canyons of Arizona

Antelope Canyon

Discover the charm of Arizona's canyons! Imagine walking through them, with sunlight creating playful beams of light and shadow. The colors are amazing, with reds, oranges, and pinks changing as the light shifts. It's like being in a natural art gallery, with each turn revealing something new.

When you hang this cross-stitch in your home, it will remind you that beauty often lies in the quiet, unexpected places. It will remind you of the beauty in transformation, much like how we grow through life's twists and turns.

Quick Facts

» Located in northern Arizona, USA.

» Formed by millions of years of water erosion.

» Sacred to the Navajo people, who have lived in the area for centuries.

Design Size	**Fabric**
» 76x76 stitches	» Aida: 14 ct
Finished Size	» Evenweave or Linen: 28 ct (stitched over 2 threads)
» On 14 ct fabric: 5.4 x 5.4 inches (13.8 x 13.8 cm)	» Color: White or Ivory
Hoop	**Thread**
» Use a 6-inch (15.2 cm) hoop for stitching and display. A 5.5-inch (13.9 cm) hoop is an option for a snug display fit.	» Type: DMC Six-strand embroidery floss
	» Usage: Stitch with 2 strands
	» Length: See Symbol Key

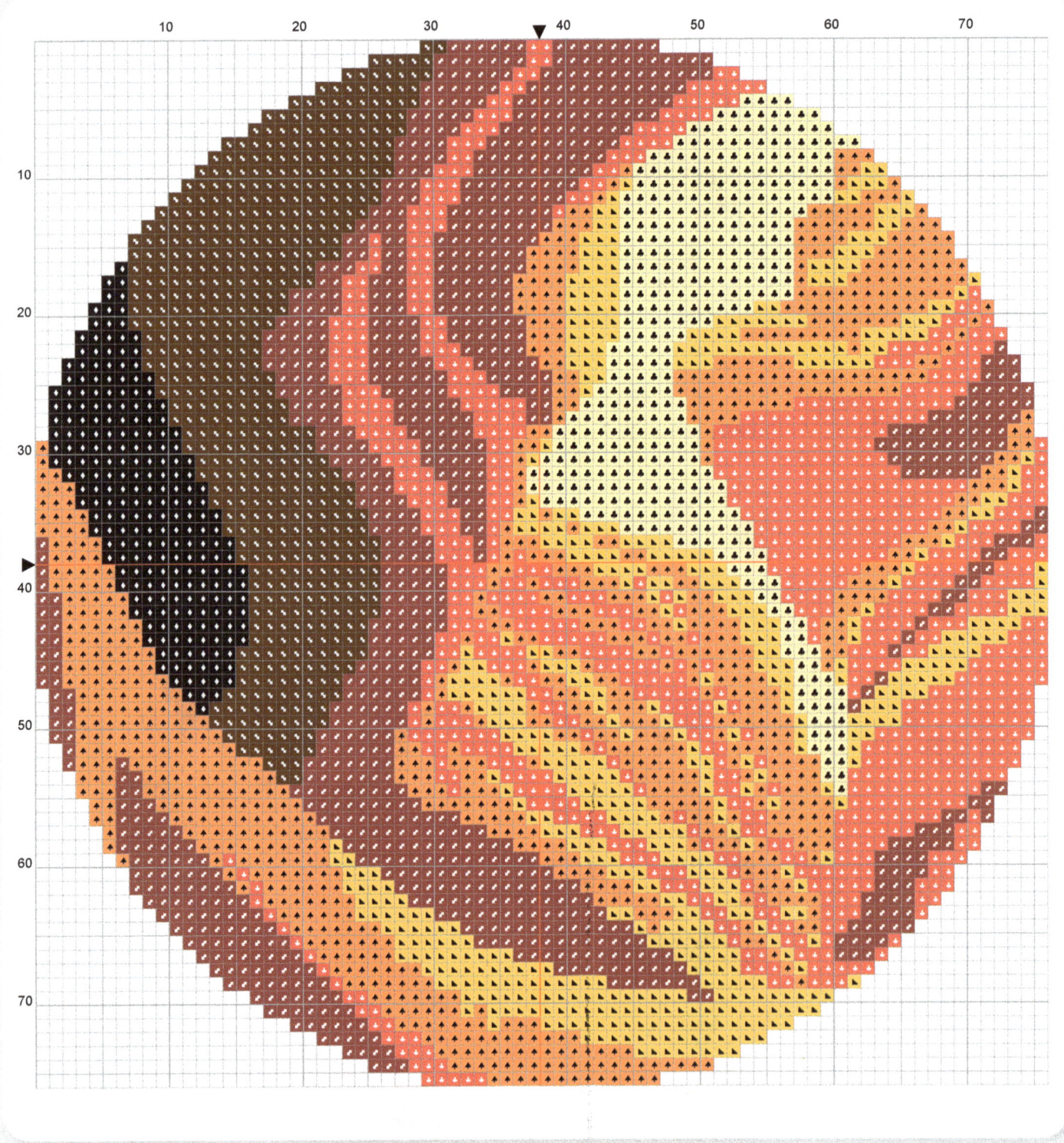

PATTERN 4

Ancient Pyramids of the Maya

Chichen Itza

The pyramids of Mexico rise from the earth like echoes of a distant past. Standing among them feels like stepping into another time—where every stone holds a story. This pattern captures the spirit of those ancient wonders, inviting you to stitch a piece of history.

As you work through the design, let it spark your sense of adventure and curiosity. It's a tribute to timeless craftsmanship and the mysteries that still linger in the ruins.

Quick Facts

» Located in the Yucatán Peninsula, Mexico.

» The main pyramid, known as El Castillo, has 91 steps on each of its four sides, totaling 365 steps—one for each day of the year.

» The structures align with celestial events, including the equinox, when shadows create the illusion of a serpent slithering down the pyramid.

Design Size
» 76x76 stitches

Finished Size
» On 14 ct fabric: 5.4 x 5.4 inches (13.8 x 13.8 cm)

Hoop
» Use a 6-inch (15.2 cm) hoop for stitching and display. A 5.5-inch (13.9 cm) hoop is an option for a snug display fit.

Fabric
» Aida: 14 ct
» Evenweave or Linen: 28 ct (stitched over 2 threads)
» Color: White or Ivory

Thread
» Type: DMC Six-strand embroidery floss
» Usage: Stitch with 2 strands
» Length: See Symbol Key

	DMC 995	DMC 700	DMC 747	DMC 906	DMC 437	DMC 945	DMC 434
Yards	34.0	4.0	8.9	16.1	8.7	10.1	9.9
Meters	31.1	3.7	8.1	14.7	8.0	9.2	9.1

PATTERN 5

Lungs of the Earth in Brazil

Amazon Rainforest

The Amazon is home to an incredible diversity of life, from jaguars and toucans to thousands of plant species that can't be found anywhere else. It's a place of endless discovery and wonder, where every step reveals something new and amazing.

For cross-stitch lovers, this pattern is a great reminder of the patience and care needed to create something beautiful, just like the rainforest has grown over countless generations. Let it remind you of the importance of nature and the beauty of our world.

Quick Facts

» Located in South America, primarily in Brazil.

» The largest rainforest in the world, covering over 5.5 million square kilometers.

» Home to an estimated 390 billion individual trees.

» Produces about 20% of the world's oxygen, earning it the nickname "Lungs of the Earth."

Design Size
» 74x74 stitches

Finished Size
» On 14 ct fabric: 5.3 x 5.3 inches (13.4 x 13.4 cm)

Hoop
» Use a 6-inch (15.2 cm) hoop for stitching and display. A 5.5-inch (13.9 cm) hoop is an option for a snug display fit.

Fabric
» Aida: 14 ct
» Evenweave or Linen: 28 ct (stitched over 2 threads)
» Color: White or Ivory

Thread
» Type: DMC Six-strand embroidery floss
» Usage: Stitch with 2 strands
» Length: See Symbol Key

	DMC 310	DMC 700	DMC 906	DMC 702	DMC 742	DMC 947	DMC 746	DMC 445
Yards	27.6	18.5	7.6	15.4	3.7	7.6	1.6	5.0
Meters	25.2	16.9	6.9	14.1	3.4	6.9	1.5	4.6

PATTERN 6

Archipelago of Evolution

Galápagos Islands

The Galápagos Islands are a living showcase of nature's creativity—home to giant tortoises, marine iguanas, and the famously quirky blue-footed boobies. Each island tells a different story of adaptation and survival.

This design highlights the iconic tortoise, a gentle symbol of resilience and evolution. With bold contrasts and thoughtful detail, the pattern invites you to stitch not just a scene, but a celebration of life's endless variety.

Quick Facts

» Located in the Pacific Ocean, about 600 miles off the coast of Ecuador.

» Consists of 18 main islands and many smaller islets.

» Famous for inspiring Charles Darwin's theory of evolution.

» The Galápagos Marine Reserve is one of the largest and most biologically diverse marine protected areas in the world.

Design Size	Fabric
» 75x75 stitches	» Aida: 14 ct
	» Evenweave or Linen: 28 ct (stitched over 2 threads)
Finished Size	» Color: White or Ivory
» On 14 ct fabric: 5.4 x 5.4 inches (13.6 x 13.6 cm)	**Thread**
	» Type: DMC Six-strand embroidery floss
Hoop	» Usage: Stitch with 2 strands
» Use a 6-inch (15.2 cm) hoop for stitching and display. A 5.5-inch (13.9 cm) hoop is an option for a snug display fit.	» Length: See Symbol Key

	DMC 310	DMC 700	DMC 958	DMC 798	DMC 433	DMC 947	DMC 742
Yards	6.4	20.4	7.3	15.0	6.8	25.7	7.7
Meters	5.9	18.7	6.7	13.7	6.2	23.5	7.0

PATTERN 7

Rapa Nui's Ancient Guardians

Easter Island

Easter Island, known as Rapa Nui, is famous for its mysterious moai statues. These ancient stone guardians, carved by the island's early inhabitants, stand tall and solemn, watching over the landscape. Each moai has its own unique features, telling stories of the ancestors they represent.

This cross-stitch design features the iconic moai statues with earthy tones. Perfect for history buffs and travel enthusiasts, this cross-stitch design makes a fantastic addition to your living room or study. It's sure to spark conversations about the fascinating mysteries of Easter Island.

Quick Facts

» Located in the southeastern Pacific Ocean, about 2,300 miles off the coast of Chile.

» Home to nearly 900 moai statues, carved from volcanic rock.

» The island is known as Rapa Nui in the native Polynesian language.

» The moai were created between 1400 and 1650 CE.

Design Size	**Fabric**
» 75x75 stitches	» Aida: 14 ct
	» Evenweave or Linen: 28 ct (stitched over 2 threads)
Finished Size	» Color: White or Ivory
» On 14 ct fabric: 5.4 x 5.4 inches (13.6 x 13.6 cm)	**Thread**
Hoop	» Type: DMC Six-strand embroidery floss
» Use a 6-inch (15.2 cm) hoop for stitching and display. A 5.5-inch (13.9 cm) hoop is an option for a snug display fit.	» Usage: Stitch with 2 strands
	» Length: See Symbol Key

	DMC 958	DMC 905	DMC 433	DMC 906	DMC 435	DMC 828	DMC 947	DMC 601	DMC 783	DMC Ecru
Yards	5.1	4.5	11.2	6.0	12.5	38.2	4.4	2.2	1.6	3.7
Meters	4.7	4.1	10.2	5.5	11.4	34.9	4.0	2.0	1.5	3.4

PATTERN 8

Circle of Ancient Stones

Stonehenge

Stonehenge has stood quietly in the English countryside for thousands of years, its massive stones arranged in a way that still sparks curiosity and awe. There's something timeless about its presence—mysterious, balanced, and deeply rooted in the earth.

This pattern captures that iconic silhouette with soft, natural tones that reflect the landscape. It's a gentle tribute to ancient wisdom and the quiet strength found in simplicity.

Quick Facts

» Located in Wiltshire, England, about 90 miles west of London.

» Believed to have been constructed between 3000 BC and 2000 BC.

» The stones are aligned with the sunrise on the summer solstice and the sunset on the winter solstice, indicating a possible connection to ancient rituals.

Design Size	**Fabric**
» 76x76 stitches	» Aida: 14 ct
Finished Size	» Evenweave or Linen: 28 ct (stitched over 2 threads)
» On 14 ct fabric: 5.4 x 5.4 inches (13.8 x 13.8 cm)	» Color: White or Ivory
Hoop	**Thread**
» Use a 6-inch (15.2 cm) hoop for stitching and display. A 5.5-inch (13.9 cm) hoop is an option for a snug display fit.	» Type: DMC Six-strand embroidery floss
	» Usage: Stitch with 2 strands
	» Length: See Symbol Key

	DMC 700	DMC 958	DMC 581	DMC 964	DMC 435	DMC 676
Yards	10.1	32.0	24.6	6.6	7.1	11.2
Meters	9.2	29.3	22.5	6.0	6.5	10.2

PATTERN 9

Alpine Majesty of Switzerland

The Alps

The Swiss Alps are a picture-perfect blend of towering peaks, quiet villages, and crisp mountain air. Cowbells echo through the valleys, and snow-capped summits stretch into the sky—it's a place where time slows and beauty surrounds you.

This pattern captures that alpine serenity, with details that evoke cozy moments and breathtaking views. As you stitch, imagine wandering through peaceful trails and sipping cocoa by the fire—your own little escape into the heart of the mountains.

Quick Facts

» Located in central Europe, spanning several countries.

» Home to some of the highest peaks in Europe, including the famous Matterhorn.

» Hidden within the Alps are stunning glacier caves, where you can walk through ice tunnels and see breathtaking blue ice formations.

Design Size
» 76x76 stitches

Finished Size
» On 14 ct fabric: 5.4 x 5.4 inches (13.8 x 13.8 cm)

Hoop
» Use a 6-inch (15.2 cm) hoop for stitching and display. A 5.5-inch (13.9 cm) hoop is an option for a snug display fit.

Fabric
» Aida: 14 ct
» Evenweave or Linen: 28 ct (stitched over 2 threads)
» Color: White or Ivory

Thread
» Type: DMC Six-strand embroidery floss
» Usage: Stitch with 2 strands
» Length: See Symbol Key

PATTERN 10

Thundering Curtain of Water

Victoria Falls

Victoria Falls, known locally as Mosi-oa-Tunya—"The Smoke That Thunders"—is a breathtaking display of nature's power and grace. Straddling the border of Zambia and Zimbabwe, its mist and roar create a scene that's both dramatic and unforgettable.

This pattern features the strength and movement of the cascading water, using flowing lines and bold contrasts to reflect its energy. As you stitch, let the rhythm of the falls inspire you—a reminder of nature's grandeur and the beauty found in its wildest places.

Quick Facts

» Located on the Zambezi River, right on the border between Zambia and Zimbabwe.

» One of the largest waterfalls in the world, about a mile wide and 354 feet high.

» Named after Queen Victoria by explorer David Livingstone, who first saw the falls in 1855.

Design Size
» 75x75 stitches

Finished Size
» On 14 ct fabric: 5.4 x 5.4 inches (13.6 x 13.6 cm)

Hoop
» Use a 6-inch (15.2 cm) hoop for stitching and display. A 5.5-inch (13.9 cm) hoop is an option for a snug display fit.

Fabric
» Aida: 14 ct
» Evenweave or Linen: 28 ct (stitched over 2 threads)
» Color: White or Ivory

Thread
» Type: DMC Six-strand embroidery floss
» Usage: Stitch with 2 strands
» Length: See Symbol Key

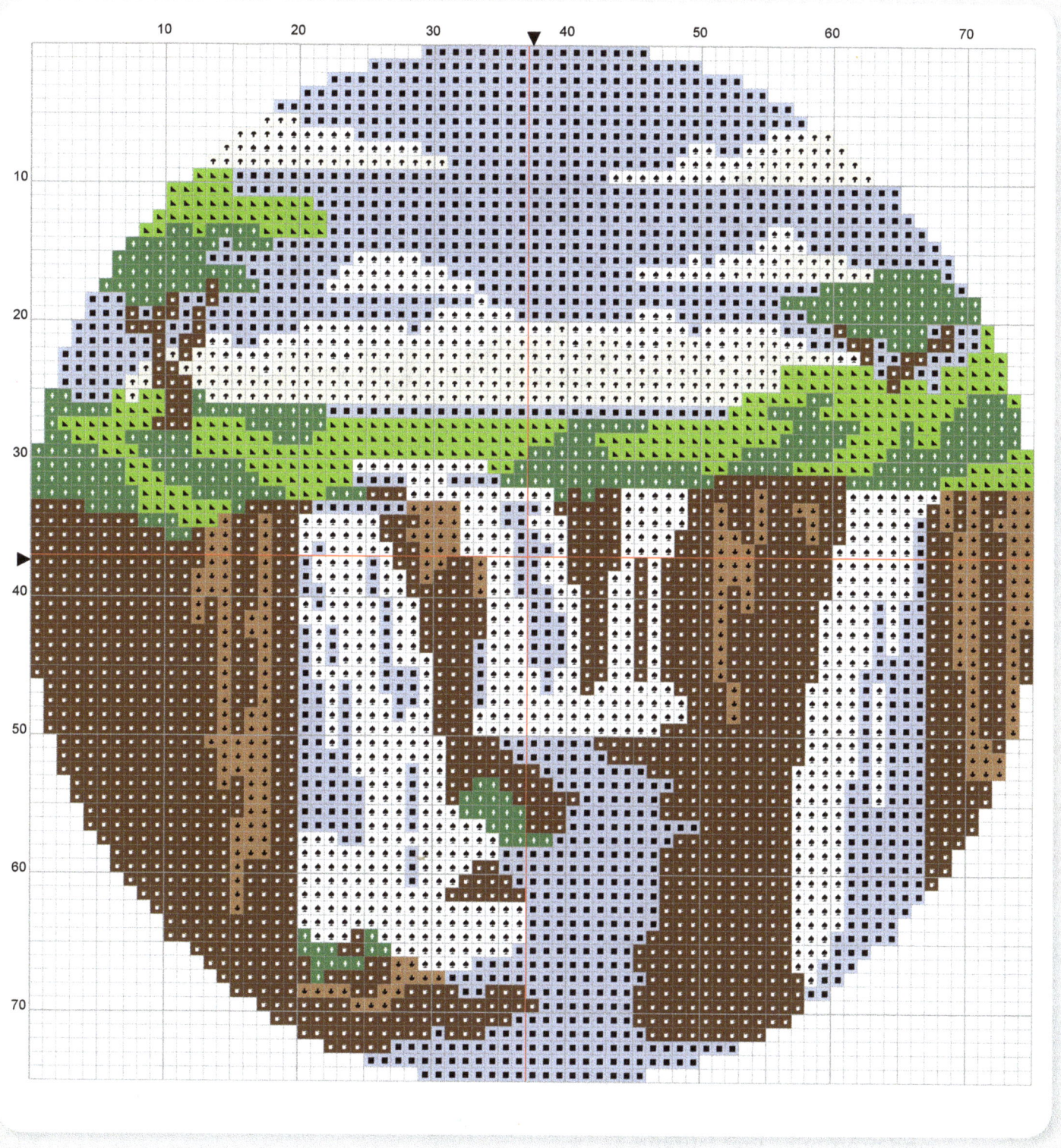

DMC 156	DMC B5200	DMC 700	DMC Ecru	DMC 435	DMC 906	DMC 801
Yards 26.3	15.4	6.9	5.1	4.2	6.0	25.6
Meters 24.0	14.1	6.3	4.7	3.8	5.5	23.4

PATTERN 11

Endless Plains of the Tanzanian Wild

Serengeti

The Serengeti at sunset is pure magic—golden skies, quiet plains, and silhouettes of giraffes moving gently through the trees. It's a moment of stillness and wonder, where nature feels both vast and intimate.

This pattern depicts a peaceful scene, with graceful giraffes and iconic acacia trees bathed in warm tones. As you stitch, let it transport you to the heart of the wild—a place where beauty unfolds slowly and memories last a lifetime.

Quick Facts

» Located in northern Tanzania, the Serengeti covers over 5,700 square miles, making it one of the largest national parks in Africa.

» The park is famous for the Great Migration, where over a million wildebeest and thousands of zebras travel in search of greener pastures.

» The name "Serengeti" comes from the Maasai word "Siringet," meaning "endless plains."

Design Size
» 76x76 stitches

Finished Size
» On 14 ct fabric: 5.4 x 5.4 inches (13.8 x 13.8 cm)

Hoop
» Use a 6-inch (15.2 cm) hoop for stitching and display. A 5.5-inch (13.9 cm) hoop is an option for a snug display fit.

Fabric
» Aida: 14 ct
» Evenweave or Linen: 28 ct (stitched over 2 threads)
» Color: White or Ivory

Thread
» Type: DMC Six-strand embroidery floss
» Usage: Stitch with 2 strands
» Length: See Symbol Key

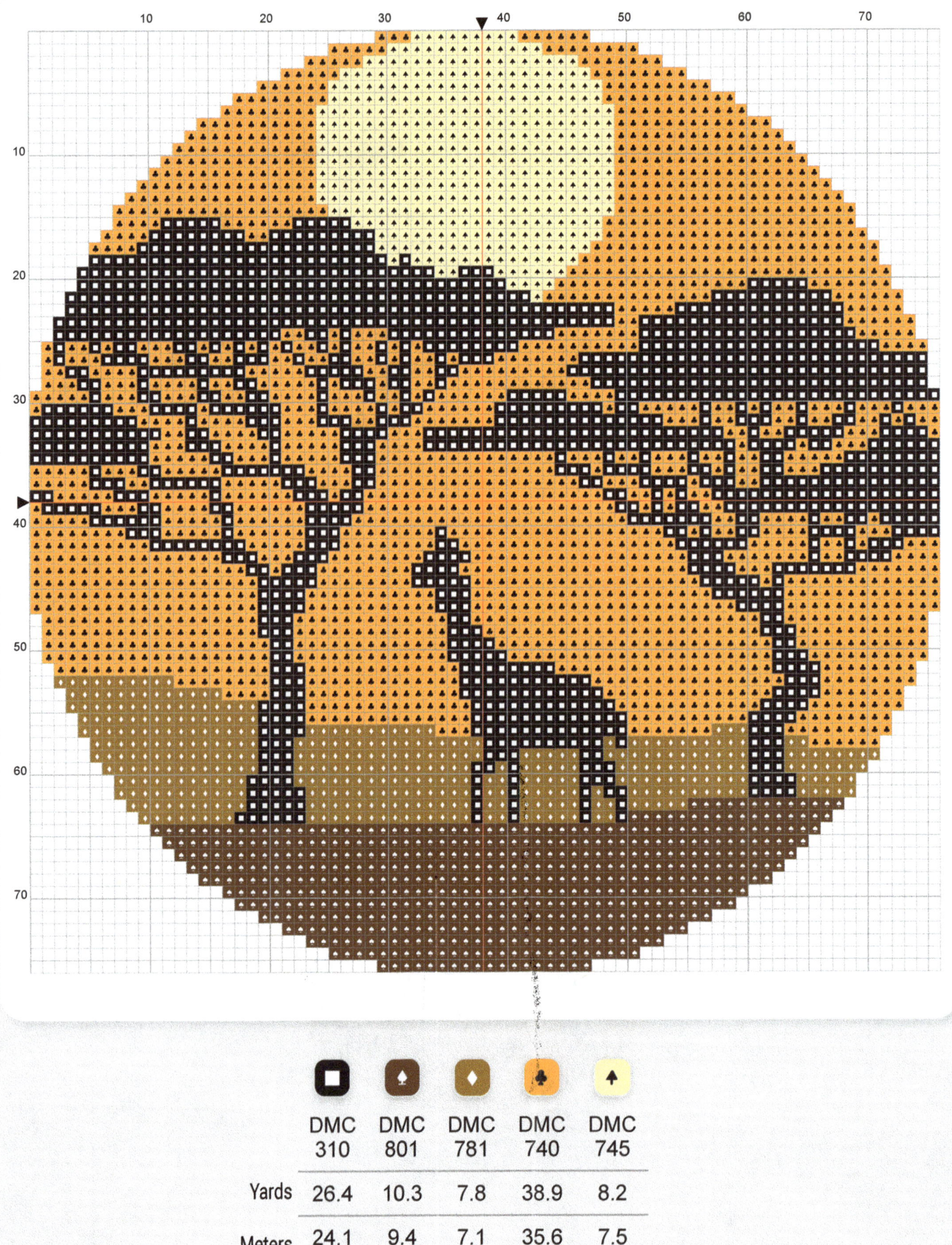

> **PATTERN 12**

Golden Crescent Shore of Sydney

Bondi Beach

Have you ever wished you could capture the essence of a perfect beach day? Bondi Beach, located in Sydney, Australia, is renowned for its golden sands and beautiful crescent-shaped shoreline. Loved by both locals and visitors, it's the perfect spot to relax, surf, and soak up the sun.

This design captures the vibrant energy of Bondi Beach with golden sands and beautiful waves. It's a reminder of the fun and relaxation found at the beach. Perfect for your living room or as a gift, it will inspire a sense of joy and tranquility in everyone who sees it.

Quick Facts

» Eastern suburbs of Sydney, about 7 km from the city center. Bondi Beach was made a public beach in 1882, making it one of the oldest public beaches in Australia.

» The beach is famous for the TV show "Bondi Rescue," which follows the daily lives and heroic rescues of the Bondi lifeguards.

Design Size
» 76x76 stitches

Finished Size
» On 14 ct fabric: 5.4 x 5.4 inches (13.8 x 13.8 cm)

Hoop
» Use a 6-inch (15.2 cm) hoop for stitching and display. A 5.5-inch (13.9 cm) hoop is an option for a snug display fit.

Fabric
» Aida: 14 ct
» Evenweave or Linen: 28 ct (stitched over 2 threads)
» Color: White or Ivory

Thread
» Type: DMC Six-strand embroidery floss
» Usage: Stitch with 2 strands
» Length: See Symbol Key

PATTERN 13

Scenic Coastal Journey of Victoria

Great Ocean Road

The Great Ocean Road winds along Australia's southern coast, offering breathtaking views of rugged cliffs, turquoise waters, and the iconic limestone stacks rising from the sea. It's a drive that leaves you feeling both humbled and refreshed.

This pattern shows the essence of that coastal beauty—waves in motion, stone formations standing tall, and a sense of calm woven into every stitch. Let it bring the ocean breeze and wide-open skies into your stitching space.

Quick Facts

» Stretches for about 243 kilometers (151 miles) along the southeastern coast of Victoria, from Torquay to Allansford.

» Home to diverse wildlife, including koalas, kangaroos, and various bird species.

» The limestone stacks are constantly shaped by the powerful waves and wind, creating new formations over time.

Design Size
» 76x76 stitches

Finished Size
» On 14 ct fabric: 5.4 x 5.4 inches (13.8 x 13.8 cm)

Hoop
» Use a 6-inch (15.2 cm) hoop for stitching and display. A 5.5-inch (13.9 cm) hoop is an option for a snug display fit.

Fabric
» Aida: 14 ct
» Evenweave or Linen: 28 ct (stitched over 2 threads)
» Color: White or Ivory

Thread
» Type: DMC Six-strand embroidery floss
» Usage: Stitch with 2 strands
» Length: See Symbol Key

DMC 156	DMC 958	DMC 995	DMC 310	DMC 3853	DMC 435	DMC 801	DMC 437	DMC 700	DMC Ecru
Yards 13.6	7.5	22.6	2.3	4.4	15.4	4.2	12.9	2.9	5.9
Meters 12.4	6.9	20.7	2.1	4.0	14.1	3.8	11.8	2.7	5.4

PATTERN 14

Limestone Spires of Nambung

Pinnacles Desert

The Pinnacles Desert in Western Australia feels like another world—golden sands scattered with ancient limestone spires that rise like silent sculptures. It's a landscape that sparks curiosity and wonder.

This design captures the quiet beauty of that surreal terrain. With each stitch, you'll recreate the calm and mystery of the desert, bringing a little piece of nature's magic into your space.

Quick Facts

» Located in Nambung National Park, about 200 kilometers (124 miles) north of Perth.

» The spires are made from ancient seashells that turned into limestone over millions of years.

» Even in the desert, you can find hardy shrubs and wildflowers, especially after winter rains.

» The Pinnacles are important to the Indigenous Yued people, who have a deep connection to this land.

Design Size
» 76x76 stitches

Finished Size
» On 14 ct fabric: 5.4 x 5.4 inches (13.8 x 13.8 cm)

Hoop
» Use a 6-inch (15.2 cm) hoop for stitching and display. A 5.5-inch (13.9 cm) hoop is an option for a snug display fit.

Fabric
» Aida: 14 ct
» Evenweave or Linen: 28 ct (stitched over 2 threads)
» Color: White or Ivory

Thread
» Type: DMC Six-strand embroidery floss
» Usage: Stitch with 2 strands
» Length: See Symbol Key

	DMC 433	DMC 781	DMC 3853	DMC 945	DMC 644	DMC 745
Yards	9.9	11.0	33.9	14.8	13.5	8.5
Meters	9.1	10.1	31.0	13.5	12.3	7.8

PATTERN 15

Jagged Peaks of Queenstown

The Remarkables

The Remarkables, near Queenstown, New Zealand, live up to their name—sharp, soaring peaks that cut into the sky and cradle serene valleys below. It's a landscape that feels both bold and peaceful, perfect for outdoor wanderers and quiet dreamers alike.

This design features that rugged charm, with crisp lines and calming tones that echo the mountain's strength and grace. Stitch by stitch, it brings a touch of alpine adventure into your home.

Quick Facts

» The Remarkables are located near Queenstown on the South Island of New Zealand.

» These mountains are composed mainly of schist, giving them their dramatic and rugged appearance.

» The Remarkables hold special significance to the local Māori people, who have many legends and stories about these majestic peaks.

Design Size
» 76x76 stitches

Finished Size
» On 14 ct fabric: 5.4 x 5.4 inches (13.8 x 13.8 cm)

Hoop
» Use a 6-inch (15.2 cm) hoop for stitching and display. A 5.5-inch (13.9 cm) hoop is an option for a snug display fit.

Fabric
» Aida: 14 ct
» Evenweave or Linen: 28 ct (stitched over 2 threads)
» Color: White or Ivory

Thread
» Type: DMC Six-strand embroidery floss
» Usage: Stitch with 2 strands
» Length: See Symbol Key

PATTERN 16

Mystic Spheres of Moeraki

Moeraki Boulders

On a quiet stretch of beach, large, round boulders rest along the shore as if placed there by a giant hand. These are the Moeraki Boulders, natural formations that have captivated visitors for generations. Found on New Zealand's South Island, these stones hold a quiet mystery that sparks the imagination.

Legend has it that the boulders are the remains of eel baskets, gourds, and kumara (sweet potatoes) that washed ashore from the great canoe, Araiteuru. This intriguing story, passed down through generations of the local Māori people, adds a layer of mystique to these stones.

Quick Facts

» Located on Koekohe Beach, along the Otago coast of New Zealand's South Island.

» These boulders formed millions of years ago, through a process called concretion, where minerals deposited around a core over time.

» Some boulders are up to 2 meters (6.5 feet) in diameter and can weigh several tons.

Design Size
» 75x75 stitches

Finished Size
» On 14 ct fabric: 5.4 x 5.4 inches (13.6 x 13.6 cm)

Hoop
» Use a 6-inch (15.2 cm) hoop for stitching and display. A 5.5-inch (13.9 cm) hoop is an option for a snug display fit.

Fabric
» Aida: 14 ct
» Evenweave or Linen: 28 ct (stitched over 2 threads)
» Color: White or Ivory

Thread
» Type: DMC Six-strand embroidery floss
» Usage: Stitch with 2 strands
» Length: See Symbol Key

PATTERN 17

Emerald Isle of the Pacific

Bora Bora

In the heart of the Pacific Ocean lies Bora Bora, an island so beautiful it seems almost mythical. With its clear turquoise waters and lush green mountains, Bora Bora has been called the "Pearl of the Pacific." But beyond its scenery, this island holds stories as captivating as its landscapes.

According to ancient Polynesian legend, Bora Bora was the first island to emerge after Raiatea, created by the gods with great care and attention. The island was originally named "Pora Pora," meaning "first born." Over time, the name evolved into the more familiar "Bora Bora."

Quick Facts

» Bora Bora is part of French Polynesia, located in the South Pacific, northwest of Tahiti.

» The island is surrounded by a lagoon and a barrier reef.

» The island's coral reefs are home to a variety of marine life, including colorful fish, rays, and sharks.

» Bora Bora has a rich cultural heritage, with traditional Polynesian music, dance, and crafts still practiced by the local community.

Design Size
» 76x76 stitches

Finished Size
» On 14 ct fabric: 5.4 x 5.4 inches (13.8 x 13.8 cm)

Hoop
» Use a 6-inch (15.2 cm) hoop for stitching and display. A 5.5-inch (13.9 cm) hoop is an option for a snug display fit.

Fabric
» Aida: 14 ct
» Evenweave or Linen: 28 ct (stitched over 2 threads)
» Color: White or Ivory

Thread
» Type: DMC Six-strand embroidery floss
» Usage: Stitch with 2 strands
» Length: See Symbol Key

	DMC 310	DMC 798	DMC 445	DMC 958	DMC 995	DMC 964	DMC 745
Yards	5.4	7.2	6.7	11.8	19.8	31.8	8.8
Meters	4.9	6.6	6.1	10.8	18.1	29.1	8.0

PATTERN 18

Volcanic Isle of Antarctica

Deception Island

Welcome to Deception Island, a truly unique spot in Antarctica! This island is actually a volcano with a natural harbor, surrounded by icy cliffs and dark, volcanic beaches. It's a place where ice and fire meet, creating a landscape like no other. The island is home to seals, penguins, and many seabirds. The waters around the island are sometimes warmed by geothermal activity, creating small, cozy spots in the otherwise chilly sea.

In this cross-stitch pattern, you'll capture the simple beauty of Deception Island: the cool blues and whites of the ice, the deep sea water, and the warm hues of a polar sunset. It's a perfect project for anyone who loves nature's surprises and the serene beauty of Antarctica.

Quick Facts

» Part of the South Shetland Islands, off the coast of Antarctica.

» Deception Island is a caldera of an active volcano, with a natural harbor known as Port Foster.

» It has been a site for whaling, scientific research, and exploration since the early 19th century.

Design Size
» 76x76 stitches

Finished Size
» On 14 ct fabric: 5.4 x 5.4 inches (13.8 x 13.8 cm)

Hoop
» Use a 6-inch (15.2 cm) hoop for stitching and display. A 5.5-inch (13.9 cm) hoop is an option for a snug display fit.

Fabric
» Aida: 14 ct
» Evenweave or Linen: 28 ct (stitched over 2 threads)
» Color: White or Ivory

Thread
» Type: DMC Six-strand embroidery floss
» Usage: Stitch with 2 strands
» Length: See Symbol Key

PATTERN 19

Sacred Summit of Japan

Mount Fuji

Japan is a land of rich culture, delicious cuisine, and stunning landscapes. One of its most famous landmarks is Mount Fuji. Its perfectly symmetrical cone has made it a symbol of beauty.

Mount Fuji is surrounded by beautiful lakes, forests, and hot springs. Mount Fuji is surrounded by beautiful lakes, forests, and hot springs. Each area offers a unique view of the mountain, making it a photographer's paradise.

In this cross-stitch pattern, you'll capture the simple beauty of Mount Fuji: the gentle slopes, the serene snow, and the peaceful surroundings. It's a perfect project for anyone who loves nature's calm and the timeless beauty of Japan.

Quick Facts

» Located on Honshu Island, about 100 kilometers southwest of Tokyo.

» Mount Fuji stands at 12,388 feet (3,776 meters), making it the highest mountain in Japan.

» Mount Fuji is an active stratovolcano, with its last eruption occurring in 1707.

» The mountain is considered one of Japan's "Three Holy Mountains" and has been a pilgrimage site for centuries.

Design Size
» 76x76 stitches

Finished Size
» On 14 ct fabric: 5.4 x 5.4 inches (13.8 x 13.8 cm)

Hoop
» Use a 6-inch (15.2 cm) hoop for stitching and display. A 5.5-inch (13.9 cm) hoop is an option for a snug display fit.

Fabric
» Aida: 14 ct
» Evenweave or Linen: 28 ct (stitched over 2 threads)
» Color: White or Ivory

Thread
» Type: DMC Six-strand embroidery floss
» Usage: Stitch with 2 strands
» Length: See Symbol Key

PATTERN 20

Limestone Jewels of Vietnam

Ha Long Bay

Ha Long Bay is a place of quiet enchantment—emerald waters, towering limestone karsts, and hidden caves that seem carved by time itself. Floating villages drift peacefully between the formations, adding to the bay's dreamlike charm.

This pattern depicts the serene beauty of the landscape, from the dramatic cliffs to the gentle ripples below. It's a calming project for anyone drawn to nature's elegance and the timeless allure of Vietnam's coastal wonders.

Quick Facts

» Ha Long Bay is located in northeastern Vietnam, in the Gulf of Tonkin.

» The bay features over 1,600 limestone islands and islets, formed over millions of years.

» Traditional floating fishing villages, such as Cua Van and Vung Vieng, offer a glimpse into the local way of life.

Design Size
» 76x76 stitches

Finished Size
» On 14 ct fabric: 5.4 x 5.4 inches (13.8 x 13.8 cm)

Hoop
» Use a 6-inch (15.2 cm) hoop for stitching and display. A 5.5-inch (13.9 cm) hoop is an option for a snug display fit.

Fabric
» Aida: 14 ct
» Evenweave or Linen: 28 ct (stitched over 2 threads)
» Color: White or Ivory

Thread
» Type: DMC Six-strand embroidery floss
» Usage: Stitch with 2 strands
» Length: See Symbol Key

	DMC 700	DMC 964	DMC 958	DMC 905	DMC 747
Yards	23.2	26.7	16.3	11.3	14.2
Meters	21.2	24.4	14.9	10.3	13.0

PATTERN 21

Island of Gods in Indonesia

Bali

Bali is a place where serenity and spirit intertwine. Nestled beside a quiet lake, Tamblingan Temple feels like a hidden sanctuary—surrounded by lush greenery, gentle breezes, and the soft hum of nature. Locals tend to the temple with quiet reverence, sharing stories passed down through generations. It's a place that invites reflection and calm.

This pattern reflects that peaceful scene, with soft details that honor the temple's beauty and its serene surroundings. As you stitch, let the calm of Bali and the warmth of its culture fill your space with quiet joy.

Quick Facts

» Bali is an Indonesian island located between Java and Lombok.

» Bali is often called the "Island of the Gods" due to its rich spiritual culture and hundreds of temples.

» Tamblingan Temple is dedicated to the Hindu deities, showcasing traditional Balinese craftsmanship.

Design Size
» 75x75 stitches

Finished Size
» On 14 ct fabric: 5.4 x 5.4 inches (13.6 x 13.6 cm)

Hoop
» Use a 6-inch (15.2 cm) hoop for stitching and display. A 5.5-inch (13.9 cm) hoop is an option for a snug display fit.

Fabric
» Aida: 14 ct
» Evenweave or Linen: 28 ct (stitched over 2 threads)
» Color: White or Ivory

Thread
» Type: DMC Six-strand embroidery floss
» Usage: Stitch with 2 strands
» Length: See Symbol Key

PATTERN 22

Buddhist Majesty in Java

Borobudur

In the heart of Java sits Borobudur, a collection of Buddhist temples. This ancient wonder isn't just one building, but many - creating a massive, stepped pyramid structure that seems to grow right out of the jungle. As you climb the levels, you're walking through a stone storybook. Each terrace is covered in intricate carvings telling tales of Buddha's life and teachings.

People from all over the world come to explore these temples. Some come to pray, others to learn, but everyone leaves with a sense of wonder. As you stitch this pattern, imagine joining them at sunrise, when the first light touches the ancient stones and brings centuries of history to life.

Quick Facts

» Located in central Java, Indonesia

» Built in the 8th–9th century during the Syailendra Dynasty

» Composed of over 2 million volcanic stone blocks

» Serves as a pilgrimage site symbolizing the journey to enlightenment

Design Size
» 75x75 stitches

Finished Size
» On 14 ct fabric: 5.4 x 5.4 inches (13.6 x 13.6 cm)

Hoop
» Use a 6-inch (15.2 cm) hoop for stitching and display. A 5.5-inch (13.9 cm) hoop is an option for a snug display fit.

Fabric
» Aida: 14 ct
» Evenweave or Linen: 28 ct (stitched over 2 threads)
» Color: White or Ivory

Thread
» Type: DMC Six-strand embroidery floss
» Usage: Stitch with 2 strands
» Length: See Symbol Key

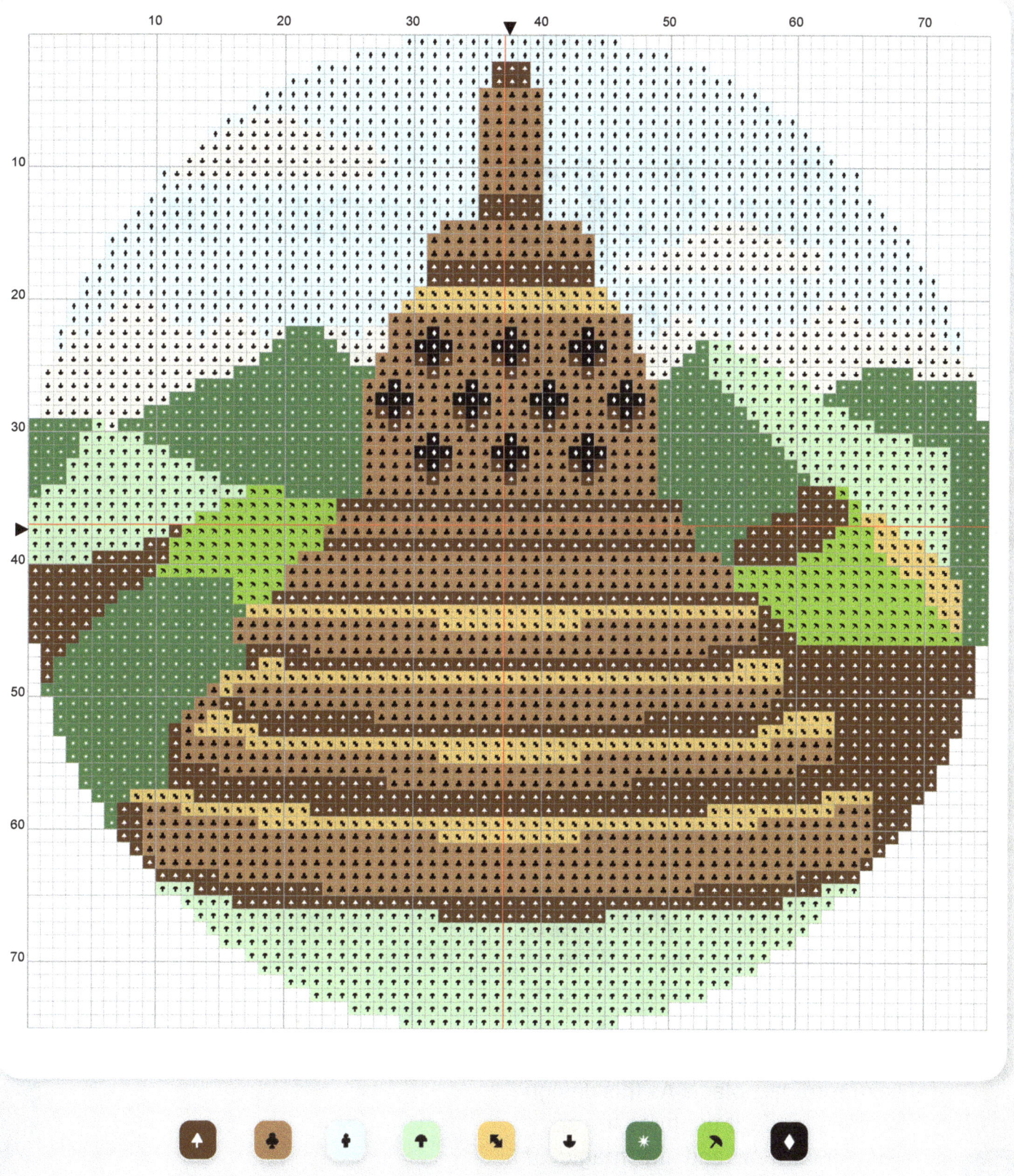

PATTERN 23

Land of Dragons in Indonesia

Komodo National Park

Komodo National Park is a destination known for its unique wildlife and landscapes. Home to the famous Komodo dragon, the world's largest lizard, the park offers a rare opportunity to observe these creatures in their natural habitat.

This cross-stitch pattern reflects the beauty of Komodo National Park, featuring the iconic dragons. Each stitch represents the adventure and wonder of this extraordinary place. As this design comes to life, it captures the spirit of exploration and the magic of nature.

Quick Facts

» Located in Indonesia, between the islands of Sumbawa and Flores

» Home to over 2,500 Komodo dragons, a vulnerable species

» Diverse marine life includes vibrant coral reefs and various fish species

Design Size
» 76x76 stitches

Finished Size
» On 14 ct fabric: 5.4 x 5.4 inches (13.8 x 13.8 cm)

Hoop
» Use a 6-inch (15.2 cm) hoop for stitching and display. A 5.5-inch (13.9 cm) hoop is an option for a snug display fit.

Fabric
» Aida: 14 ct
» Evenweave or Linen: 28 ct (stitched over 2 threads)
» Color: White or Ivory

Thread
» Type: DMC Six-strand embroidery floss
» Usage: Stitch with 2 strands
» Length: See Symbol Key

	DMC 742	DMC 310	DMC 801	DMC 445	DMC 700	DMC 317	DMC 666
Yards	15.1	7.8	18.6	16.1	14.1	7.6	12.4
Meters	13.8	7.1	17.0	14.7	12.9	6.9	11.3

PATTERN 24

Lion Rock Fortress of Lanka

Sigiriya

Sigiriya, an ancient rock fortress in Sri Lanka, is a remarkable testament to the island's rich history and architectural brilliance. Constructed in the 5th century by King Kasyapa, the fortress served as both a royal citadel and a monastic retreat. Legend has it that Kasyapa chose this strategic location to escape his father's wrath and to protect himself from his half-brother, who sought to reclaim the throne.

This cross-stitch pattern focuses on the large rock plateau of Sigiriya, showcasing its impressive height and unique shape. As you work on this pattern, think about the stories this rock has seen over the years, the gardens that once bloomed around it, and the lives of the people who lived there.

Quick Facts

» Located in the central province of Sri Lanka

» Built in the 5th century by King Kasyapa as a royal citadel

» Surrounded by well-designed gardens and water features

Design Size
» 76x76 stitches

Finished Size
» On 14 ct fabric: 5.4 x 5.4 inches (13.8 x 13.8 cm)

Hoop
» Use a 6-inch (15.2 cm) hoop for stitching and display. A 5.5-inch (13.9 cm) hoop is an option for a snug display fit.

Fabric
» Aida: 14 ct
» Evenweave or Linen: 28 ct (stitched over 2 threads)
» Color: White or Ivory

Thread
» Type: DMC Six-strand embroidery floss
» Usage: Stitch with 2 strands
» Length: See Symbol Key

PATTERN 25

Volcanic Beauty of Jeju

Jeju Island

Jeju Island is famous for its unique volcanic landscapes. Known as the "Island of the Gods," it features beautiful beaches, lush hills, and Hallasan Mountain, the tallest peak in South Korea. Visitors can hike its trails, enjoying breathtaking views and discovering hidden waterfalls.

This cross-stitch pattern captures the essence of Jeju's volcanic beauty, showcasing its diverse landscapes and natural wonders. As this design comes together, it brings to life the peacefulness of Jeju and the warmth of its culture.

Quick Facts

» Located off the southern coast of South Korea

» Known for its volcanic origin and stunning landscapes

» Features unique geological formations like lava tubes and craters

Design Size
» 76x76 stitches

Finished Size
» On 14 ct fabric: 5.4 x 5.4 inches (13.8 x 13.8 cm)

Hoop
» Use a 6-inch (15.2 cm) hoop for stitching and display. A 5.5-inch (13.9 cm) hoop is an option for a snug display fit.

Fabric
» Aida: 14 ct
» Evenweave or Linen: 28 ct (stitched over 2 threads)
» Color: White or Ivory

Thread
» Type: DMC Six-strand embroidery floss
» Usage: Stitch with 2 strands
» Length: See Symbol Key

PATTERN 26

Dragon's Backbone of China

Great Wall

The Great Wall of China, known as the "Dragon's Backbone," stretches for miles across beautiful landscapes. This ancient structure winds through mountains and valleys, with stone and brick walls rising and falling with the terrain, resembling a dragon across the earth. Watchtowers dot the horizon, adding to its charm.

Constructed starting in the 7th century BC, the wall symbolizes strength and hard work. It tells the stories of the people who built it, from soldiers to farmers. As you stitch this pattern, envision the winding path and the watchtowers that once held guards. Each stitch reflects the beauty and history of this remarkable landmark.

Quick Facts

» Stretches across northern China

» It served as a defense against invasions and a means of communication.

» It's estimated that over a million workers contributed to the construction, many of whom were conscripted laborers.

Design Size
» 76x76 stitches

Finished Size
» On 14 ct fabric: 5.4 x 5.4 inches (13.8 x 13.8 cm)

Hoop
» Use a 6-inch (15.2 cm) hoop for stitching and display. A 5.5-inch (13.9 cm) hoop is an option for a snug display fit.

Fabric
» Aida: 14 ct
» Evenweave or Linen: 28 ct (stitched over 2 threads)
» Color: White or Ivory

Thread
» Type: DMC Six-strand embroidery floss
» Usage: Stitch with 2 strands
» Length: See Symbol Key

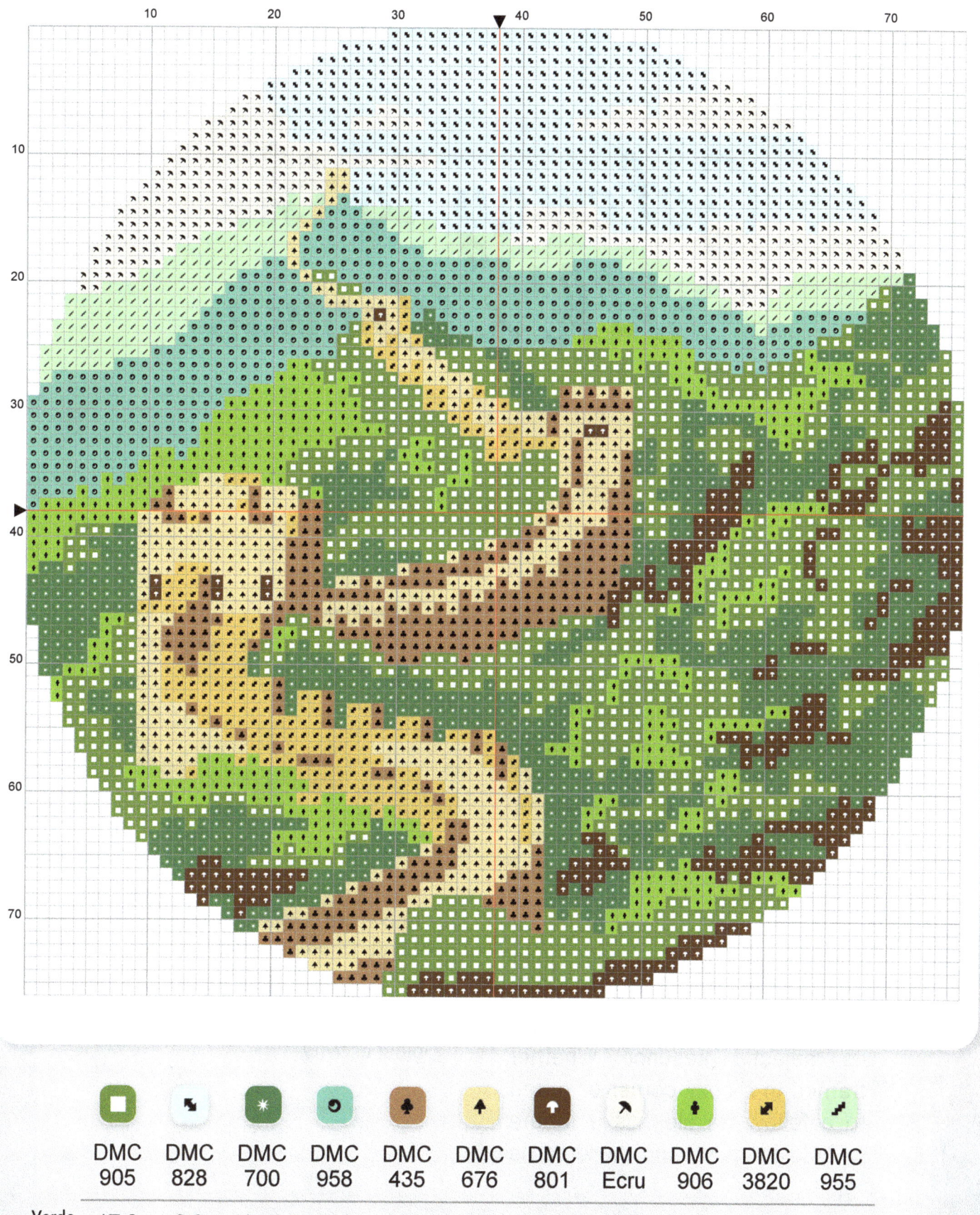

	DMC 905	DMC 828	DMC 700	DMC 958	DMC 435	DMC 676	DMC 801	DMC Ecru	DMC 906	DMC 3820	DMC 955
Yards	17.8	9.9	14.6	8.5	6.1	7.4	5.6	6.0	7.9	4.0	3.9
Meters	16.3	9.1	13.4	7.8	5.6	6.8	5.1	5.5	7.2	3.7	3.6

PATTERN 27

Gateway to the Earth's Crown

Mount Everest

Mount Everest rises above the world at 29,032 feet—a breathtaking symbol of resilience, ambition, and the spirit of adventure. Its snow-capped summit has called to explorers and dreamers for generations, standing as a reminder of what's possible when we reach for the extraordinary.

This pattern features the quiet strength of Everest, with crisp lines and cool tones that echo its majestic presence. Whether framed in a cozy corner or gifted to a fellow traveler, it's a tribute to bold journeys and the dreams that drive them. As you stitch, let it inspire your own path—one thread at a time.

Quick Facts

» Located in the Himalayas on the border between Nepal and Tibet.

» Known as "Sagarmatha" in Nepal and "Chomolungma" in Tibet.

» The mountain grows about 4 millimeters each year due to geological activity.

Design Size
» 76x76 stitches

Finished Size
» On 14 ct fabric: 5.4 x 5.4 inches (13.8 x 13.8 cm)

Hoop
» Use a 6-inch (15.2 cm) hoop for stitching and display. A 5.5-inch (13.9 cm) hoop is an option for a snug display fit.

Fabric
» Aida: 14 ct
» Evenweave or Linen: 28 ct (stitched over 2 threads)
» Color: White or Ivory

Thread
» Type: DMC Six-strand embroidery floss
» Usage: Stitch with 2 strands
» Length: See Symbol Key

	DMC 156	DMC 801	DMC 798	DMC 742	DMC 746	DMC 700
Yards	32.5	12.7	9.7	8.2	25.6	2.7
Meters	29.7	11.6	8.9	7.5	23.4	2.5

PATTERN 28

Fairy Chimneys and Hidden Valleys

Cappadocia

Cappadocia is a land of wonder—where whimsical rock formations rise from the earth and hot air balloons drift through the morning sky. Carved by centuries of wind and time, its valleys and cave dwellings tell stories of ancient life and quiet magic.

This pattern shows the charm of dawn in Cappadocia, with soft colors and graceful shapes that echo the region's beauty. Whether stitched for yourself or gifted to a fellow traveler, it's a gentle tribute to adventure, imagination, and the joy of discovering someplace truly unique.

Quick Facts

» Located in central Turkey.

» The region has a rich history, with ancient cave dwellings and churches carved into the soft volcanic rock.

» Known for its underground cities, which were used for refuge during invasions.

Design Size
» 76x76 stitches

Finished Size
» On 14 ct fabric: 5.4 x 5.4 inches (13.8 x 13.8 cm)

Hoop
» Use a 6-inch (15.2 cm) hoop for stitching and display. A 5.5-inch (13.9 cm) hoop is an option for a snug display fit.

Fabric
» Aida: 14 ct
» Evenweave or Linen: 28 ct (stitched over 2 threads)
» Color: White or Ivory

Thread
» Type: DMC Six-strand embroidery floss
» Usage: Stitch with 2 strands
» Length: See Symbol Key

PATTERN 29

Salt Lake of Tranquility

The Dead Sea

The Dead Sea has been a place of wonder for centuries. Ancient Egyptians and Romans traveled to its shores to enjoy its healing waters, believing they could cure various ailments. This special lake, located between Jordan and Israel, is famous for its high salt content, which lets people float effortlessly on its surface.

This cross stitch piece would be a lovely addition to any home, celebrating the unique beauty of this natural wonder. It also makes a thoughtful gift for anyone who loves nature and tranquility.

Quick Facts

» Located between Jordan and Israel.

» The Dead Sea is the lowest point on Earth, sitting around 1,410 feet below sea level.

» The Dead Sea is shrinking due to water diversion and mineral extraction.

Design Size
» 76x76 stitches

Finished Size
» On 14 ct fabric: 5.4 x 5.4 inches (13.8 x 13.8 cm)

Hoop
» Use a 6-inch (15.2 cm) hoop for stitching and display. A 5.5-inch (13.9 cm) hoop is an option for a snug display fit.

Fabric
» Aida: 14 ct
» Evenweave or Linen: 28 ct (stitched over 2 threads)
» Color: White or Ivory

Thread
» Type: DMC Six-strand embroidery floss
» Usage: Stitch with 2 strands
» Length: See Symbol Key

	DMC Ecru	DMC 728	DMC 964	DMC 644	DMC 3853	DMC 954	DMC 435	DMC 958	DMC 798	DMC 995	DMC 745
Yards	13.5	13.8	12.6	9.3	7.0	9.1	5.7	7.3	5.2	4.4	3.8
Meters	12.3	12.6	11.5	8.5	6.4	8.3	5.2	6.7	4.8	4.0	3.5

PATTERN 30

Colorful Underwater Paradise

The Red Sea

This cross stitch pattern is inspired by the beauty of the Red Sea. Famous for its vibrant coral reefs and diverse marine life, this sea is a paradise for snorkelers and divers. The underwater world is filled with colorful fish, sea turtles, and fascinating coral formations. As you stitch this pattern, imagine the joy of swimming among the vibrant marine life and feeling the warm sun overhead.

This cross stitch piece would make a wonderful addition to any home, celebrating the beauty of the sea. It also makes a great gift for anyone who loves the ocean or dreams of underwater adventures.

Quick Facts

» Located between northeastern Africa and the Arabian Peninsula.

» The region has a rich history, with ancient trade routes and shipwrecks to explore.

Design Size
» 76x76 stitches

Finished Size
» On 14 ct fabric: 5.4 x 5.4 inches (13.8 x 13.8 cm)

Hoop
» Use a 6-inch (15.2 cm) hoop for stitching and display. A 5.5-inch (13.9 cm) hoop is an option for a snug display fit.

Fabric
» Aida: 14 ct
» Evenweave or Linen: 28 ct (stitched over 2 threads)
» Color: White or Ivory

Thread
» Type: DMC Six-strand embroidery floss
» Usage: Stitch with 2 strands
» Length: See Symbol Key

	DMC 995	DMC 954	DMC 435	DMC 676	DMC Ecru	DMC 666	DMC 353	DMC B5200	DMC 581
Yards	9.0	13.5	7.2	18.0	15.5	2.3	18.0	4.4	3.9
Meters	8.2	12.3	6.6	16.5	14.2	2.1	16.5	4.0	3.6

Thread Conversion

DMC	Anchor
156	118
310	403
317	400
351	10
353	6
433	358
434	310
435	1046
437	362
445	288
581	280
601	57
606	334
644	830
666	46
676	891
700	211
702	225
704	237
728	305
740	316
742	303
745	300
746	275
747	158
781	308
783	307
798	131
801	359
816	20
828	975
905	257
906	256
945	881
947	330
954	203
955	206
957	50
958	187
964	1092
972	298
995	410
3348	264
3747	120
3820	306
3853	1003
B5200	1
Ecru	387

Colors may not match exactly between brands. Check your threads before stitching to get the look you want.

All designs and illustrations in this book are original creations inspired by global landscapes and cultural heritage. No official affiliations or endorsements are implied.

Copyright © 2025 by Lily Ann

All rights reserved. No part of this book may be reproduced, distributed, or transmitted in any form or by any means, including photocopying, recording, or other electronic or mechanical methods, without the prior written permission of the author, except as permitted by copyright law.

Selling Finished Works

You may sell finished cross-stitch works created with these patterns on a small, handmade scale (e.g., craft fairs, online shops). However, you cannot resell or distribute the patterns themselves in any form. Mass production or factory manufacturing is prohibited without written permission from the author.

Disclaimer

Every effort has been made to ensure that all instructions are accurate and safe; however, the author and publisher disclaim any liability for any injury, damage, or loss that may result from the use of the patterns or instructions in this book.

Published by My Cute Patterns

Printed in the United States of America

First Edition: September 2025

www.ingramcontent.com/pod-product-compliance
Lightning Source LLC
Chambersburg PA
CBHW080551030426
42337CB00024B/4830